KNIGHT

MARC TYLER NOBLEMAN

Chicago, Illinois

© 2008 Raintree
Published by Raintree,
A division of Reed Elsevier Inc.
Chicago, Illinois

Customer Service 888-454-2279

Visit our website at www.heinemannraintree.com

Designed by Victoria Bevan and Bigtop
Printed and bound in China by Leo Paper Group

12 11 10 09 08
10 9 8 7 6 5 4 3 2

**Library of Congress
Cataloging-in-Publication Data**
Nobleman, Marc Tyler.
 Knight / Marc Tyler Nobleman.
    p. cm.
 Includes bibliographical references and index.
 ISBN 978-1-4109-2971-6 (library binding-
hardcover) -- ISBN
978-1-4109-2992-1 (pbk.)
 1. Knights and knighthood--Juvenile literature. I.
Title.
 CR4509.N63 2008
 940.1--dc22

       2007003393

Acknowledgments
The author and publisher are grateful to the
following for permission to reproduce copyright
material: Alamy Images (Skyscan Photolibrary)
p. **21**; The Art Archive pp. **6** (bottom) (Musée
du Château de Versailles/Dagli Orti), **6** (top)
(Bodleian Library, Oxford), **10** (Musée des Arts
Décoratifs Paris/Dagli Ort); Bridgeman Art Library
pp. **5** (Private collection/Chris Beetles, London,
UK), **13** (Russell-Cotes Art Gallery and Museum,
Bournemouth, UK), **22** (Ken Welsh/Private
Collection), **25** (top) (Private Collection/Look and
Learn); Corbis pp. **9** (Darama), **14** (The Art Archive),
17 (Christie's Images), **26** (Images.com), **29** (top)
(Tim Graham Picture Library); Kobal Collection
pp. **25** (bottom) (20th Century Fox/Lucasfilm), **29**
(bottom) (Miramax Films/Universal Pictures/
Laurie Sparham).

Cover photograph of a knight reproduced with
permission of Getty Images (Taxi).

Photo research by Hannah Taylor
Illustration by Ron Wilson

The publishers would like to thank Nancy Harris,
Diana Bentley, and Dee Reid for their assistance in
the preparation of this book.

Contents

Some words are printed in bold, **like this**. You can find out what they mean in the glossary. You can also look in the box at the bottom of the page where the word first appears.

WHAT IS A KNIGHT?

Two men on horseback thunder toward each other across a battlefield. They raise their weapons and then CLANG! With dented armor, both circle around for another hit.

Various warriors throughout history are known as knights. For many people, the most familiar type is the European knight of the **Middle Ages**. These **medieval** knights began to appear around the year 1000. They had to ride a horse, use weapons such as swords, and wear heavy armor—all at the same time!

Whom did knights serve?

Medieval kings divided their kingdoms into smaller areas ruled by **lords**. Knights usually served one lord and, in return, they were sometimes paid in gifts of land.

lord	man who rules others
medieval	relating to the Middle Ages
Middle Ages	era of European history commonly dated from the 400s to the 1500s

Knights served their lords in battle 40 days a year—sometimes more during wartime.

Fascinating fact!

Some boys became knights because their fathers were knights.

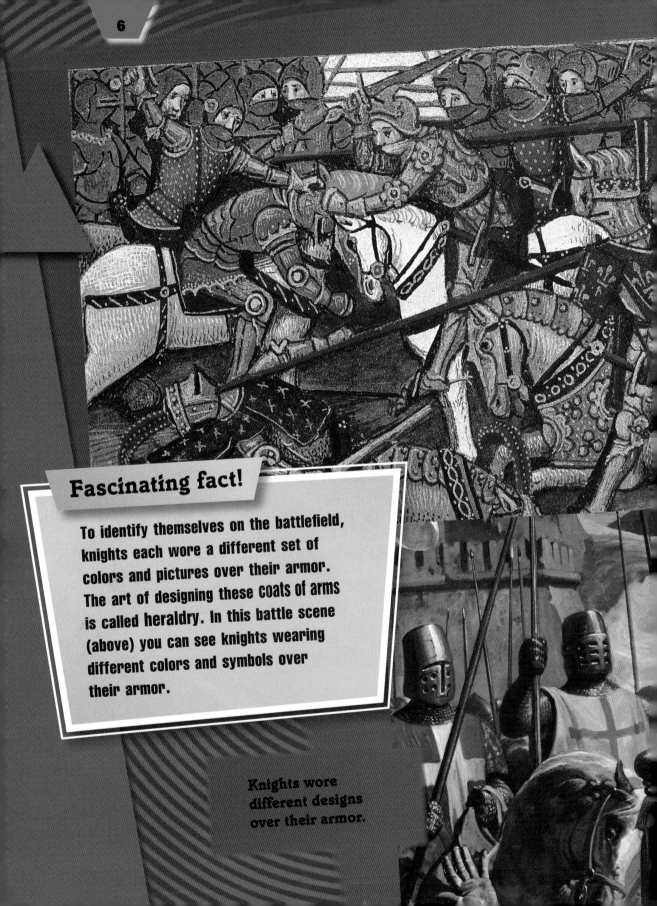

Fascinating fact!

To identify themselves on the battlefield, knights each wore a different set of colors and pictures over their armor. The art of designing these coats of arms is called heraldry. In this battle scene (above) you can see knights wearing different colors and symbols over their armor.

Knights wore different designs over their armor.

WHAT DID KNIGHTS DO?

A knight's job was to protect his lord from enemies.

Medieval European kingdoms did not have armies of paid soldiers. Instead, knights often fought on their own, staying close to their lords' castles to defend them. They battled invaders from other lands, or even the knights of other lords.

Did knights ever team up?

Sometimes knights banded together for a common cause. Two religious groups both wanted control of the holy city of Jerusalem. One group was Christian, the other was Muslim. Thousands of knights traveled there to seize the city for Christianity. These wars were called the **Crusades**.

coat of arms	symbol or design of a particular family
Crusades	medieval wars between Christians and Muslims
heraldry	art of creating family symbols or designs

KNIGHTS IN SHINING ARMOR

Knights usually fought one another on horseback, but sometimes they fought on foot. Either way, they needed protection.

Medieval knights wore armor made from small, linked metal rings. This **chain mail** could protect a knight from the slash of a sword. It was also flexible, so a knight could move in it.

Did knights wear other armor?

When enemies began to use **longbows** and **crossbows** that could pierce chain mail, knights began to wear **plate armor**. It was stronger but heavier than chain mail. They put plate armor on piece by piece, building a shining suit. However, knights still wore chain mail over armpits and other places that plate armor could not easily cover.

chain mail	armor made of small metal rings
crossbow	weapon that shoots an arrow called a bolt
longbow	large, powerful bow for shooting arrows
plate armor	armor made of large pieces of metal

Fascinating fact!

A knight's armor could weigh up to 60 pounds (27 kilograms).

head: armet (a visored helmet that fully covered the head)

shoulder: pauldron

mouth and chin: bevor

upper arm: rerebrace

hand: gauntlet

lower arm: vambrace

elbow: couter

torso: cuirass

waist and hips: chain mail

mace

dagger

sword

crossbow

Knights usually fought on horseback using a range of weapons, from swords to **crossbows.**

WHAT WEAPONS DID KNIGHTS HAVE?

A knight's most important weapon was also his friend—a horse!

On horseback, knights could charge at enemies quickly, jabbing them with sharp poles called **lances**. Lances were often more than 10 feet (3 meters) long. Some knights trained their horses to **rear up** and kick enemy soldiers who were fighting on foot.

A knight's main handheld weapon was his sword. When not using it, he kept it in a leather **scabbard** attached to his waist.

What smaller weapons did knights use?

Knights carried knives called daggers that were small enough to stab between pieces of **plate armor**. Knights also swung steel **maces** and axes to crush enemy armor.

lance	pole a knight used to knock another knight off his horse
mace	club that sometimes had spikes on it
rear up	when a horse stands on its back two legs and raises its front two legs
scabbard	case for holding a sword

How Did A Boy Become A Knight?

In some families, young sons were sent away to train to become knights. The training would last from age seven until adulthood.

What are pages and squires?

These boys became **pages** for knights. A page served food and ran errands, while also learning to fight and hunt. Meanwhile, the women of the knight's family educated pages about manners, music, and religion.

At age 14 a page might become a **squire**. Squires were assistants to knights. They tended to a knight's horses and cleaned his armor and weapons. They helped their master knight prepare for battle and went along to observe fighting techniques.

Fascinating fact!

Sons of **noble** birth often learned to ride a pony by age five.

Pages practiced with wooden **lances** and swords that had blunt (not sharp) tips.

noble   wealthy, important person

page   young boy serving a knight

squire   teenage boy in training to be a knight

Sometimes a knight was dubbed with only one other knight present. Other times a crowd watched and celebrated.

A **squire** who did well could become a knight when he was between 18 and 21 years old.

On the eve of the knighting ceremony, a squire's hair was cut short. He **fasted** and prayed through the night. In the morning, he bathed and dressed in fine clothes.

What happened during the dubbing ceremony?

The squire knelt before a standing knight, who touched the flat part of a sword to the squire's shoulder or neck. This ceremony is called **dubbing**. The squire was then a knight. A knight could also dub a squire during a battle.

Fascinating fact!

Some squires could not afford to become knights because horses and armor were too expensive.

dubbing	ceremony in which a person becomes a knight
fast	stop eating for a period of time

CHIVALRY

A knight promised to follow a code of good behavior called chivalry.

Chivalry meant he should demonstrate bravery in battle, defend women, and protect the weak and poor. He should also respect the church, and be loyal to his **lord**.

Were knights always chivalrous?

Many knights were indeed chivalrous, but they were often violent, too. Slicing off limbs and smashing in heads were part of the job. Some knights were brutal to **commoners**. They demanded **ransoms** of gold and silver to release their prisoners.

chivalry	knight's code for good behavior
commoner	person who has no special title
joust	contest between two knights on horseback
ransom	money paid in order to free prisoners

Fascinating fact!

Before jousts, a lady might give a knight her scarf. He would wear it during the joust to honor her.

The thick outer wall and moat surrounding a stone castle made it difficult for enemies to attack!

tower

portcullis

drawbridge

moat

CASTLE LIFE

A castle is a building that was home to a king or a **lord** and his family. The people who worked for him, including knights, also lived there.

How did castles protect lords?

Though castles were homes, their main purpose was protection. Knights were on duty at all times. Some castles were surrounded by a deep ring of water called a moat. To let visitors cross the water, a large, flat platform called a drawbridge could be lowered over it and raised afterward. A portcullis was a metal gate blocking the entrance to the castle. Castles were first constructed from wood, then later from stone.

Fascinating fact!

Castles usually contain a prison called a dungeon. Dungeons are often underground, but some are in high towers.

Castles could be cold, dark, and damp. There were usually few windows, though there were many rooms, including a great hall for large feasts.

Everything castle residents needed was built on the **grounds**. This commonly included wells, gardens, horse stables, and even a church.

What is a motte and bailey?

A motte and bailey is an early type of castle. A motte is a small hill surrounded by a ditch. A bailey is a large yard surrounded by a wall of logs at the base of the motte. A **lord** built a house called a **keep** on the motte, while villagers built homes on the bailey.

Fascinating fact!

Some knights spent more time at their lords' castles than on their own land.

| grounds | land surrounding a castle |
| keep | home of a lord in a motte and bailey castle |

Jousts were competitions, but sometimes they ended in death. If a lance struck a knight through his armor or helmet he would be very badly injured, if not killed.

THE SPORT OF KNIGHTS

When knights were not fighting, they might be showing off. Underneath vivid, fluttering banners, they competed in tournaments before cheering crowds.

In a **joust**, two knights rode at each other, aiming to knock each other off their horses with a **lance**. If both succeeded, they sometimes continued fighting on the ground.

Were jousts dangerous?

Jousts were good practice for knights—but they were also dangerous. **Lords** did not want to lose their knights in jousts, but knights sometimes did get killed. To lower the chance of death, knights in certain jousts used lances that were not sharp.

| tournament | contest for knights |

KNIGHTS BEYOND THE MIDDLE AGES

Not all knights are associated with medieval Europe.

In ancient China, warriors skilled in personal **combat** were called *xiá*. This is often translated as "knights." Like medieval European knights, *xiá* were not part of an army but rather worked alone, doing good for others.

Samurai were Japanese warriors who carried two swords. Like knights, they were **nobles** who served higher nobles. They also had codes of behavior that were similar to **chivalry**.

How are knights used in fiction?

The superhero Batman is nicknamed the Dark Knight. He fights with high-tech gear, not swords and horses.

combat fighting or battle

To avoid the shame of capture, samurai sometimes performed seppuku—killing themselves by cutting open their own bellies.

In the *Star Wars* movies, heroes with swords of light and powerful minds are called Jedi Knights.

Dragons are symbols used in **heraldry**. They appeared on shields and garments.

KNIGHT LEGENDS

Knights had adventurous lives, but some stories about them are myths.

Knights did not fight dragons. The reason is simple: dragons never existed. The scariest creatures that knights faced were other humans!

Fairy-tale knights rescue damsels in distress, but the main job of a real knight was to fight for his **lord**.

Who is King Arthur?

Stories about King Arthur and the Knights of the Round Table have been popular for centuries. Some believe King Arthur is either a legend or is based on more than one person.

MODERN KNIGHTS

Knights exist today, but they do not wear armor to work.

Certain countries still have **dubbing** ceremonies. Some people are knighted for military service, but many are knighted for other types of distinguished achievements. It is an honor to be knighted.

How is a modern knight dubbed?

In the United Kingdom, part of the dubbing ceremony has not changed for hundreds of years. The person being knighted kneels before the king or queen. The end of a sword is placed on the person's right shoulder, then the left.

Some people believe that all it takes to be a knight is bravery and courtesy. If so, there are still many knights in the world.

Fascinating fact!

Today, male knights are addressed as "Sir," such as actor Sir Ian McKellen. Female knights are addressed as "Dame."

Actress Dame Judi Dench (left) was made a real-life knight by Queen Elizabeth II.

In a movie, Dame Judi Dench played Queen Elizabeth I. She had knights of her own!

Glossary

chain mail armor made of small metal rings

chivalry knight's code for good behavior

coat of arms symbol or design of a particular family

combat fighting or battle

commoner person who has no special title

crossbow weapon that shoots an arrow called a bolt

Crusades medieval wars between Christians and Muslims

dubbing ceremony in which a person becomes a knight

fast stop eating for a period of time

grounds land surrounding a castle

heraldry art of creating family symbols or designs

joust contest between two knights on horseback

keep home of a lord in a motte and bailey castle

lance pole a knight used to knock another knight off his horse

longbow large, powerful bow for shooting arrows

lord man who rules others

mace club that sometimes had spikes on it

medieval relating to the Middle Ages

Middle Ages era of European history commonly dated from the 400s to the 1500s

noble wealthy, important person

page young boy serving a knight

plate armor armor made of large pieces of metal

ransom money paid in order to free prisoners

rear up when a horse stands on its back two legs and raises its front two legs

scabbard case for holding a sword

squire teenage boy in training to be a knight

tournament contest for knights

Want to Know More?

Books

✴ *Eye Wonder: Castle and Knight.*
New York: Dorling Kindersley,
2005.

✴ Weintraub, Aileen. *Knights:*
Warriors of the Middle Ages.
New York: Children's Press, 2005.

✴ Wilkinson, Philip. *Questions and*
Answers: Knights and Castles.
New York: Kingfisher, 2001.

Websites

✴ www.nationalgeographic.com/
features/97/castles/enter.html
Try this "Ghosts in the Castle" game.

✴ www.yahooligans.com
Type "Middle Ages" or "Crusades"
into this search engine to find out
more about this time in history, and
the battles in which knights fought.

If you liked this Atomic book, why don't you try these...?

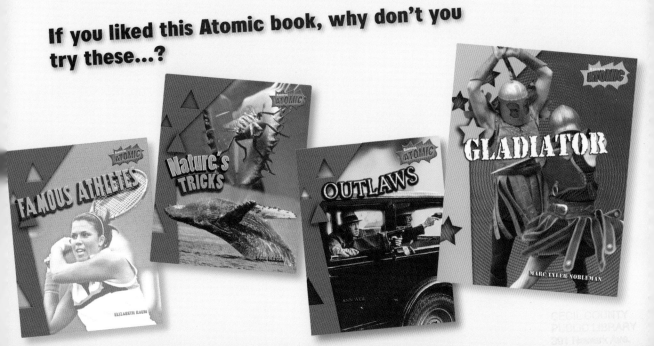

Index